ENGINEERING MARVELS
GREAT WALL OF CHINA

by Vanessa Black

pogo

Ideas for Parents and Teachers

Pogo Books let children practice reading informational text while introducing them to nonfiction features such as headings, labels, sidebars, maps, and diagrams, as well as a table of contents, glossary, and index.

Carefully leveled text with a strong photo match offers early fluent readers the support they need to succeed.

Before Reading

- "Walk" through the book and point out the various nonfiction features. Ask the student what purpose each feature serves.
- Look at the glossary together. Read and discuss the words.

Read the Book

- Have the child read the book independently.
- Invite him or her to list questions that arise from reading.

After Reading

- Discuss the child's questions. Talk about how he or she might find answers to those questions.
- Prompt the child to think more. Ask: Have you ever seen the Great Wall of China, either in person or in a photograph?

Pogo Books are published by Jump!
5357 Penn Avenue South
Minneapolis, MN 55419
www.jumplibrary.com

Library of Congress Cataloging-in-Publication Data

Names: Black, Vanessa, 1973- author.
Title: Great Wall of China / by Vanessa Black.
Description: Minneapolis, MN: Jump!, Inc., [2017]
Series: Engineering marvels | Audience: Ages 7-10.
Includes index. | Identifiers: LCCN 2017004261 (print)
LCCN 2017004785 (ebook) | ISBN 9781620317006 (hard
cover: alk. paper) | ISBN 9781624965777 (e-book)
Subjects: LCSH: Great Wall of China (China)—Juvenile
literature. | Civil engineering—China—History—Juvenile
literature. | China—History—To 221 B.C.—Juvenile
literature. | Walls—China—Design and construction—
History—Juvenile literature.
Classification: LCC DS793.G67 B53 2017 (print)
LCC DS793.G67 (ebook) | DDC 931.04—dc23
LC record available at https://lccn.loc.gov/2017004261

Editor: Kirsten Chang
Book Designer: Leah Sanders
Photo Researcher: Leah Sanders

Photo Credits: jaume/Shutterstock, cover; Martin
Puddy/Getty, 1; omers/Shutterstock, 3; aphotostory/
Shutterstock, 4-5, 16-17, 23; chinahbzyg/Shutterstock,
6-7; yesfoto/iStock, 8-9; steve estvanik/Shutterstock,
10; loco75/Thinkstock, 10; SIHASAKPRACHUM/
Shutterstock, 11; imageBROKER/SuperStock, 12-13;
Dorling Kindersley/Getty, 14-15; primopiano/
Shutterstock, 14-15; Sorapop Udomsri/Shutterstock,
14-15; Benjamas Pech/Shutterstock, 18; summer.wu/
Shutterstock, 19; David Allan Brandt/Getty, 20-21.

Printed in the United States of America at
Corporate Graphics in North Mankato, Minnesota.

TABLE OF CONTENTS

CHAPTER 1

MANY WALLS

You probably know that the Great Wall of China is a very long wall. But did you know it is the longest **structure** ever made by humans? Or that there is rice in its **mortar**?

It is an engineering marvel!

It is not actually one wall. It is many walls. The walls were built at different times with different **materials**. Many of them were then connected.

reat Wall is about 13,170
6 kilometers) long. That
ive times as long as the d
en New York City and Los

WHERE IS IT?

The Great Wall is in the northern part of China.

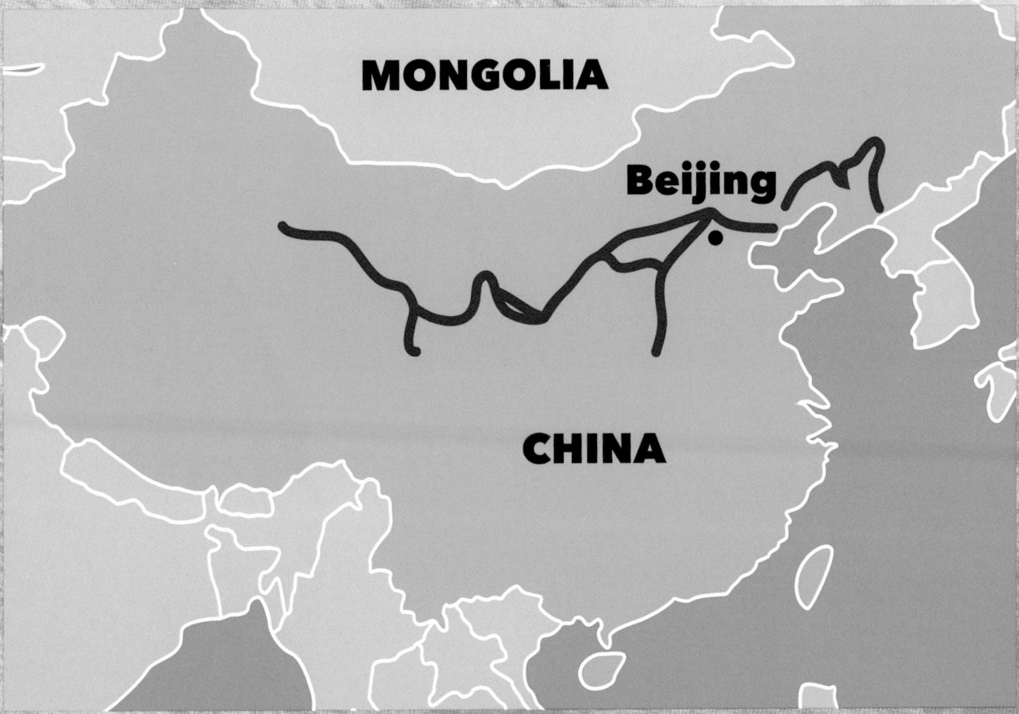

MONGOLIA

Beijing

CHINA

N
W E
S

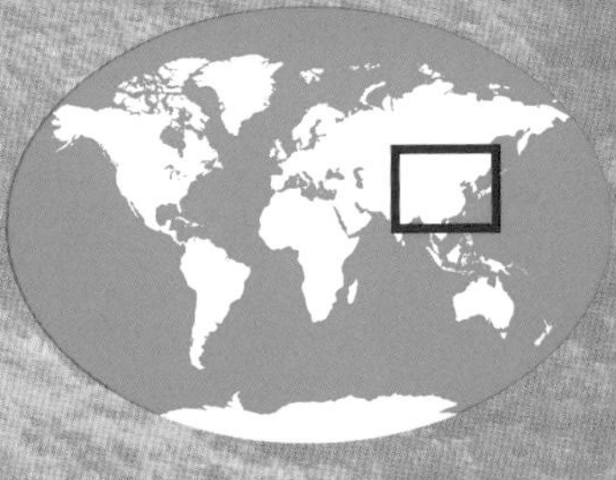

■ = Great Wall of China

CHAPTER 2

2,000 YEARS

The Great Wall was built over a period of 2,000 years. It was meant to keep out **invaders** from the north.

The first walls were simple. They were made of stone and earth. They were not very tall. They were not very strong.

In 221 B.C.E., the Emperor Qin Shi Huang oversaw construction of the first major wall. It was a huge project. It was 3,100 miles (4,988 km) long. It took a million people 10 years to build. They used a method called **hangtu**.

How do you build a hangtu wall?

1) Start by making frames using wooden poles.

2) Fill the inside of the frame with a layer of soil.

3) Pound the soil with stone tools. It should be hard-packed.

4) Lay **bamboo** or **reeds** on top of the soil. This helps it dry.

5) Repeat until the wall is as tall as the frame.

Hangtu walls are very strong. They can even survive earthquakes!

Over the next centuries, walls were built up. Some were destroyed. Others were ignored and fell apart.

Then came the Ming **dynasty** (1368–1644). The Great Wall rose to its full glory. Builders used better designs. They used brick, **limestone**, and **granite**. The walls were bigger and stronger. They rose as high as 25 feet (7.6 meters). They had forts

CHAPTER 3

OBSTACLES

Building the Great Wall was not easy. One problem was finding materials. This was hard in the desert. They used what they could find: sand!

But sand alone was not enough. Jade Gate Pass was built by layering sand and reeds. Builders had to cart in reeds from rivers far away.

Jade Gate Pass

Another problem was getting materials to the **job site**. There were no cars or trains. Workers used ox carts and wheelbarrows. It was slow. It was hard.

Building the Great Wall was a huge task. Accidents happened. People died. But in the end, the wall stands. It is an important symbol of human strength. We can stand on it and marvel!

DID YOU KNOW?

The Great Wall was built for defense. But it did not keep **Mongol** forces from invading in the 13th century and again in 1550.

ACTIVITIES & TOOLS

MAKE A MINI WALL

In this activity, you will build a miniature version of a wall out of rice mortar.

What You Need:
- white rice
- pan
- small rocks
- blender or food processor
- long piece of wood
- plastic bag with a seal

❶ With an adult, cook the rice as directed on package.

❷ Use the blender or food processor to blend the rice into a paste. This is your mortar.

❸ Put the mortar into the plastic bag. Seal it.

❹ Cut a small piece of the corner of the bag.

❺ Squeeze some mortar onto the long piece of wood.

❻ Arrange the rocks on the wood, and apply mortar between the rocks.

❼ Let dry.

GLOSSARY

bamboo: A tall, woody plant with hollow stems.

dynasty: A period of time when a particular family ruled a country.

granite: A very hard kind of rock.

hangtu: A method of building a wall in which soil is packed between a frame made of wooden poles.

invaders: People who come into another land to take it over or steal.

job site: The place where something is being built.

limestone: A type of rock that contains calcium.

materials: Things used to make or build something.

Mongol: A member of one of the peoples of the Asian country of Mongolia, north of China.

mortar: A mixture that is put between bricks to hold them together.

reeds: Tall, thin grasses.

sticky rice: A kind of starchy rice that is sticky when cooked.

structure: Something that is built by putting parts together.

INDEX

TO LEARN MORE

Learning more is as easy as 1, 2, 3.

1) Go to www.factsurfer.com
2) Enter "GreatWallofChina" into the search box.
3) Click the "Surf" button to see a list of websites.

With factsurfer, finding more information is just a click away.